ISBN-13: 978-1974027248
ISBN-10: 1974027244
First Edition: July 2017
10 9 8 7 6 5 4 3 2 1

He was born in Portugal. Growing up, his parents were quite poor. His mom worked in a garden, while his father cooked. They made barely enough to support their children.

Do you have a brother or sister? Even though you love your siblings, do you want privacy sometimes? Ronaldo didn't have that... ever. He had a brother and two sisters, and his family could only afford one room for all of them to live in. Imagine sharing a room with all of your siblings... Would you go crazy?

He looked at his hobbies and decided to dive into sports. He soon discovered that he loved to play soccer, or, as it's known in Portugal, futbul.

His determination paid off for him and he did well. As he grew older, he kept playing.

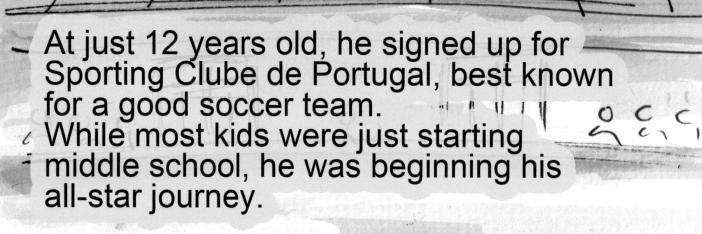

At just 12 years old, he signed up for Sporting Clube de Portugal, best known for a good soccer team.
While most kids were just starting middle school, he was beginning his all-star journey.

At 14, he dedicated his whole life to soccer. Most teenagers still had no idea what they were going to do in life, but Ronaldo had a plan, and he was going to stick to it.

At 18, he was signed into the big leagues, playing for Manchester United, where he soon became a legend.

Off the field, he still takes care of his family, and he hopes that his story can influence the next generation of children.

There are things in your life that may bring you down, and while it's hard to control them, you too should turn your hopes into your determination. Use your energy for something you're passionate about, and you too can go far... just like Ronaldo.

Made in United States
Troutdale, OR
03/23/2024

18673312R00024